LIGHTNING
BOLT
BOOKS™

Meet a Baby Tasmanian Devil

Jon M. Fishman

Lerner Publications • Minneapolis

Lerner Publications Company
A division of Lerner Publishing Group, Inc.
241 First Avenue North
Minneapolis, MN 55401 USA

For reading levels and more information, look up this title at www.lernerbooks.com.

Library of Congress Cataloging-in-Publication Data

Names: Fishman, Jon M., author.
Title: Meet a baby Tasmanian devil / Jon M. Fishman.
Description: Minneapolis : Lerner Publications, [2017] | Series: Lightning bolt books. Baby Australian animals | Audience: Ages 6-9. | Audience: K to grade 3. | Includes bibliographical references and index.
Identifiers: LCCN 2016038212 (print) | LCCN 2016050319 (ebook) | ISBN 9781512433852 (lb : alk. paper) | ISBN 9781512450576 (eb pdf)
Subjects: LCSH: Tasmanian devil—Infancy—Juvenile literature. | Tasmanian devil—Life cycles—Juvenile literature.
Classification: LCC QL737.M33 F57 2017 (print) | LCC QL737.M33 (ebook) | DDC 599.2/7139—dc23

LC record available at https://lccn.loc.gov/2016038212

Manufactured in the United States of America
1-42021-23891-10/11/2016

Table of Contents

Amazing Race

This mother Tasmanian devil is about to give birth! Her babies have been growing inside her for twenty-one days.

Baby Tasmanian devils are called imps. The mother usually gives birth to twenty to forty imps at a time. The imps are pink and don't have any hair. They cannot see or hear.

Baby Tasmanian devils are also called joeys and pups.

Each imp is about 0.4 inches (1 centimeter) long. That is the same size as a grain of rice.

The imps race about 3 inches (7.6 cm) to their mother's pouch to drink milk as soon as they are born. There are four teats inside the pouch. Only four imps can survive.

Three imps drink milk from the teats.

Family Time

The four imps stay attached to their mother's teats for about four months. Then the imps start to come out of the pouch.

The imps have hair and can hear and see when they come out of the pouch.

A mother Tasmanian devil is big enough to protect her babies from predators. She weighs about 17 pounds (8 kilograms). That is about the same weight as a six-month-old human baby.

Imps stay with their mother to be safe. Large birds might try to eat young imps.

Sometimes imps will travel with their mother. They ride on her back. Other times, imps stay in a den while their mother looks for food. Imps can also climb trees to stay safe.

Imps play with one another like puppies. They growl and screech. They wrestle and bite.

These imps are playing!

Finding Food

Imps stop drinking milk after about six months. Their mother brings them meat to eat.

Imps practice eating food. Imps eat carrion, the meat from dead animals. Tasmanian devils also hunt small animals such as mice and birds.

Two young Tasmanian devils eat a piece of meat caught by their mother.

Tasmanian devils have sharp teeth and strong jaws. Imps learn to eat every part of an animal. They even eat the bones!

Imps growl at one another over their food. They hiss and wrestle. They may have to fight for their food as adults.

Tasmanian devils hiss and growl first. They fight only if they have to.

The Single Life

Imps leave their mother at about ten months of age. They come out at night to search for food.

A Tasmanian devil can go as far as 10 miles (16 kilometers) in one night!

The Tasmanian devil stays in each den for a couple of days before moving.

A Tasmanian devil hunts and sleeps in its home range. This area can be from 2.5 to 17 square miles (6.5 to 43 sq. km). The Tasmanian devil may have several dens there.

Tasmanian devils usually
stay away from one another.
Sometimes they fight over food.

Tasmanian devils are ready to become parents when they are about two years old. They often live five to six years.

Tasmanian Devil Life Cycle

Length of pregnancy: twenty-one days

Baby Tasmanian devil comes out of pouch: four months

Life span: five to six years in the wild

Stops nursing and starts eating meat: six months

Tasmanian devil leaves its mom: ten months

Habitat in Focus

- Wild Tasmanian devils live only on the Australian island of Tasmania. They disappeared from the main Australian island hundreds of years ago.

- Tasmanian devils are in danger of dying off. Predators, disease, and vehicles all put Tasmanian devils at risk.

- Tasmanian devils live in dens under logs, bushes, and other natural places. They may also dig dens under buildings.

Fun Facts

- A Tasmanian devil's scientific name is *Sarcophilus harrisii.* That's Latin for "Harris's meat lover." In 1808, scientist George Harris wrote about Tasmanian devils.

- Tasmanian devils don't always spend all day in their dens. They have been seen lying in the sun and taking in its warmth.

- Tasmanian devils got their name from Europeans who moved to Australia. The settlers named them devils because of their loud growling and screeching.

Glossary

carrion: dead animal meat

den: a hole or other open space where an animal lives

predator: an animal that eats other animals

range: a large area where an animal lives

teat: the place on a female Tasmanian devil's body where the imps drink milk

Further Reading

Easy Science for Kids:
"Tasmanian Devils—The Land Cleaners"
http://easyscienceforkids.com/all-about
-tasmanian-devils

National Geographic Kids: Tasmanian Devil
http://kids.nationalgeographic.com/animals
/tasmanian-devil/#tasmanian-devil-red-ears
-log.jpg

Owings, Lisa. *Learning about Australia*.
Minneapolis: Lerner Publications, 2016.

Quinlan, Julia J. *Tasmanian Devils*. New York:
PowerKids, 2013.

Roza, Greg. *Tasmanian Devil vs. Hyena*. New York:
Gareth Stevens, 2016.

San Diego Zoo Kids: Tasmanian Devil
http://kids.sandiegozoo.org/animals/mammals
/tasmanian-devil

Index

Photo Acknowledgments

The images in this book are used with the permission of: © Gerry Pearce/imageBROKER/
Alamy, pp. 2, 8, 11, 22; © iStockphoto.com/Craig Dingle, pp. 4, 12, 15, 17, 19 (walking on dirt);
© Heath Holden/Getty Images, p. 5; © Auscape International Pty Ltd/Alamy, p. 6; © Roland
Seitre/Minden Pictures, p. 7; © Dave Watts/Alamy, p. 9; © D. Parer and E. Parer-Cook/
Minden Pictures, p. 10; © iStockphoto.com/Bernhard Richter, pp. 13, 18; © Gerry Pearce/
Alamy, pp. 14, 19 (in mother's pouch); © Adwo/Shutterstock.com, p. 16; © iStockphoto.com/
VMJones, p. 19 (standing in grass); © Nicholas Pitt/Alamy, p. 20.

Front cover: © Lukas Blazek/Dreamstime.com.

Main body text set in Billy Infant regular 28/36. Typeface provided by SparkType.

22.78

'3

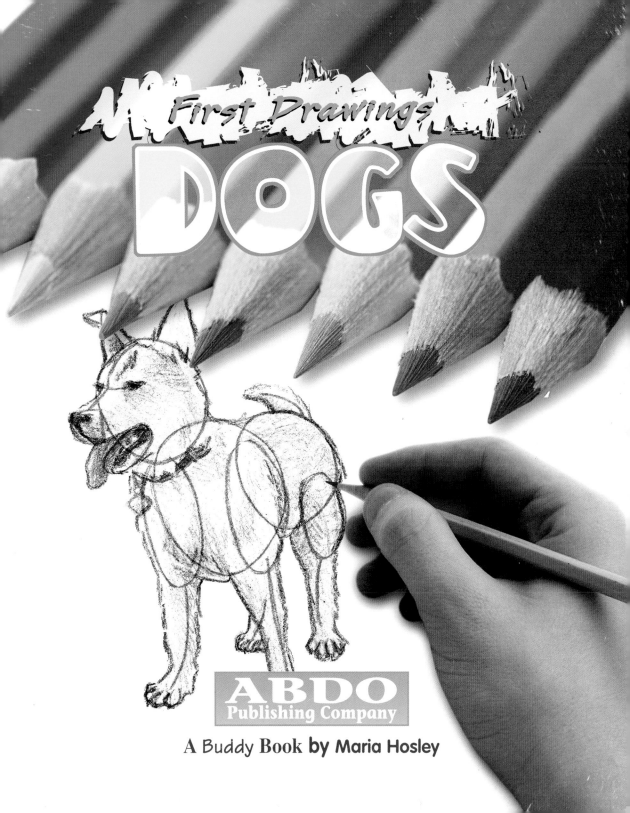

VISIT US AT

www.abdopublishing.com

Published by ABDO Publishing Company, 4940 Viking Drive, Edina, Minnesota 55435.

Copyright © 2007 by Abdo Consulting Group, Inc. International copyrights reserved in all countries. No part of this book may be reproduced in any form without written permission from the publisher. Buddy Books™ is a trademark and logo of ABDO Publishing Company.

Printed in the United States.

Editor: Sarah Tieck
Contributing Editor: Michael P. Goecke
Illustrations: Maria Hosley
Interior Photographs: Photos.com

Library of Congress Cataloging-in-Publication Data

Hosley, Maria.
  Dogs / Maria Hosley.
     p. cm. — (First drawings)
  Includes index.
  ISBN-13: 978-1-59679-803-8
  ISBN-10: 1-59679-803-3
     1. Dogs in art—Juvenile literature. 2. Drawing—Technique—Juvenile literature.
  [1. Dogs in art. 2. Drawing—Technique.] I. Title.

NC783.8.D64H67 2007
743.6'9772—dc22
                                                          2006032077

Table Of Contents

Getting Started

Today you're going to learn to draw a dog. Not sure you know how to draw? If you know how to make circles, squares, and triangles, you can draw most anything!

You will learn to draw in four steps. First, you will measure to get the correct sizes. Next, you will lightly draw the basic shapes. This helps you construct a dog. From those basic shapes, you will make the final outline. And last, you will erase the basic shape lines and add **detail**.

Can you see the basic shapes in the picture of the real dog?

To draw a dog, you'll need paper, a sharpened pencil, a big eraser, and a hard, flat surface. Many artists like to draw at a table or a desk. They sit up straight with their tools in front of them. Gather your supplies. Then, let's get started!

ARTIST'S TOOLBOX

Most dogs don't sit still long enough to be **sketched**. So, you may need to find a **reference** picture. Many artists draw from these images. Some have folders filled with them!

Start your own reference folder by collecting photographs or pictures from magazines. Then, use them as you draw. This book has a reference picture of a dog to get you started.

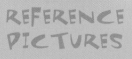

REFERENCE PICTURES

Measurements and Proportions

Have you ever looked at a drawing and thought about whether it looks real? Many people draw dogs that look like the real-life animal.

To make a **realistic** drawing of a dog, find out the dog's proportions. Proportion is the size of one thing compared to another. For example, a dog's head should be a size that fits with the rest of its body. Using correct proportions helps make your dog drawing look realistic.

There is an easy way to match the proportions of a real-life dog for your drawing. You can use strips of paper to measure the body parts on your reference picture. Here's how to do it:

Cut a strip of paper the same width as the dog's head. Then, make several more strips of the same size.

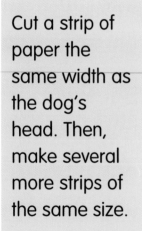

Lay the strips on the dog. Do this to compare the head size with the body width and the dog's height.

The body is about 1⅓ strips wide.

The dog's height is a little less than 3 strips.

Choosing A Size For Your Drawing

To draw this dog at this size, cut several strips of paper that match the length of the orange strips shown above.

If you want a larger drawing, cut longer strips. And if you want a smaller drawing, cut shorter strips. Just make sure the strips fit on your drawing paper.

Place your cut strips on your drawing paper. Arrange them so they match the reference picture. With your pencil, lightly mark the ends of each strip.

Make your mark short here because the dog is shorter than 3 strips.

Make your mark short here because the dog is only 1⅓ strips wide.

Basic Shapes

All things are easier to draw if you break them down into basic shapes. Draw these shapes *very lightly*. They are only a guide that you will erase later. And when the lines are light, it is easy to erase and try again. Remember to use your proportion lines as a guide!

Between your top guidelines, draw a wide oval for the face and an oval for the lower part of the mouth. Add a square to indicate the snout. Add triangles to the top of the head for the ears. Draw tall ovals for the body and the upper legs. Finally, sketch lines for the legs and the tail and ovals for the paws.

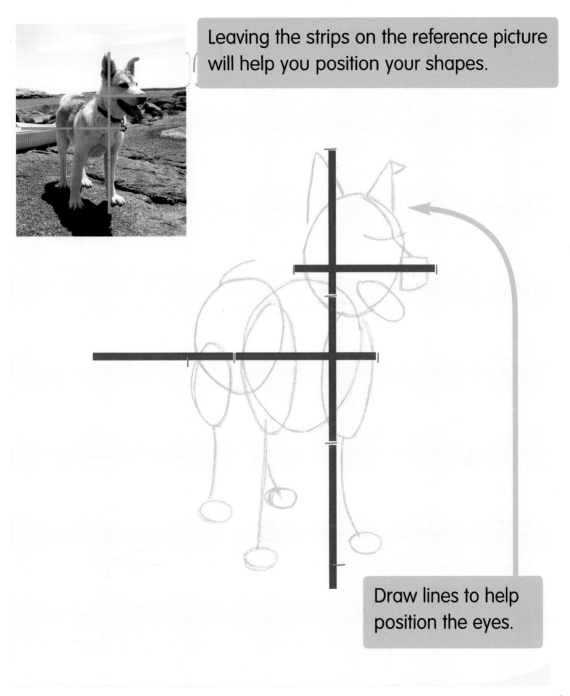

Leaving the strips on the reference picture will help you position your shapes.

Draw lines to help position the eyes.

Final Outline

Now you have drawn the basic shapes for your dog! You can use them to make the final outline shape. Do this *lightly* with a pencil.

Follow around the outside of the basic shapes to give your dog shape. Draw the legs and the tail. Add lines to shape the eyes, nose, mouth, and tongue. Put in lines for the collar and tag. Last, put in lines to define the paws.

15

Adding Detail

Once you are happy with your outline, erase the basic shape lines. Be careful not to erase any lines you still need.

Now you can add the **details**! Along the outline, add lines for the dog's hair. Draw longer hairs at the base of the ears. Then, round and shade the eyes and the nose.

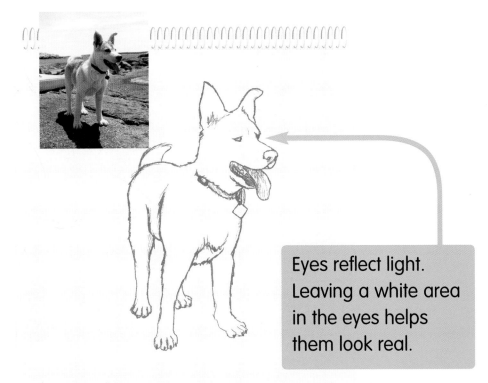

Eyes reflect light. Leaving a white area in the eyes helps them look real.

When you are happy with your outline and **details**, you can make them darker. Do this with your pencil or a marker. Erase any extra lines, and you're done!

Keep Drawing

You have now finished a drawing of a dog. Good job! Use these steps next time you want to draw something.

Don't worry if drawing feels like a challenge at first. Like anything else, drawing takes practice.

Have fun with your new skills. And remember to practice, practice, practice! The more you draw the better you will become.

Want to keep challenging yourself? Try using crayons to add color to your dog. Add a background to your drawing, too.

19

Use a black crayon to darken the outlines. Use several shades of tan and brown to create the hair. Draw those lines in the same direction that the dog's hair grows.

Caricature Dogs

It is fun to **exaggerate** parts of the dog. This is how you make a caricature. A caricature is a picture that looks like a cartoon.

Choose one body part or feature of the dog. Then, exaggerate it to make it look funny. Just use your imagination!

You can make a dog have human facial **expressions**. Practice drawing dog faces that show emotion. Then, try making your dog's body position match its mood.

PROUD

shocked

content

Using the same basic shapes, we created a caricature of the dog. We made the legs shorter and the eyes larger. We moved the front legs farther apart and gave him a smile. Then, we added motion lines for a wagging tail. These details make him look eager to play.

Important Words

detail a minor decoration, such as the longer hair in a dog's ears.

exaggerate to make something seem larger or different than it really is.

expression a look that shows feeling.

realistic showing things as they are in real life.

reference a picture or an item used for information or help.

sketch to make a rough drawing.

snout a part of the face, including the nose and the mouth, that sticks out. Some animals, such as dogs, have a snout.

Web Sites

To learn more about drawing dogs, visit ABDO Publishing Company on the World Wide Web. Web site links about drawing dogs are featured on our Book Links page. These links are routinely monitored and updated to provide the most current information available.

www.abdopublishing.com

Index